# *SCHOOL NA SCAM:* Solving the Myth of Schooling and Wealth Generation.

Bolaji A. Samuel

# Table of Contents

# INTRODUCTION

*"In our own school years, most of us were subjected not to a system of education, but to a system of ELIMINATION".*
-Robert Kiyosaki

For us Nigerians, the statement that makes up the title of this book became a trend towards the close of 2019 and the midyear of 2020. A lot of people saw the shortcomings of formal education, but it is much more important to note that most of those who made or backed this statement were either unserious (with their lives); earning money illegally, or had never attended the four walls of the classroom.

Another set of those who ever made this statement are those who have done their dues with attending school; they might have even done well in school, yet they have not come out to do well in life.

I am not and will not in any way be a proponent of the cancellation of formal education as I have had my share of the same. Yet, I would not love to sit by and help to propagate a gospel that has in many ways not worked for me.

Formal education itself will always be good, it is just that the system adopted by formal educators and policymakers will never work for anyone. As Robert Kiyosaki called it, "...a system of elimination"; like ancient Geneticist – Charles Darwin made attestations to the fact that during a period of evolution, the 'fittest survives while the weakest never do'; the school system has also become the same.

We have adopted making point blank opinions that those who do not do great with our subject matters are the weak ones; by so doing, we turned the whole class into a tripartite organization; which are:

1. 1st – 3rd positions as Prize winners

2. 4th – 50th positions as Striving to thrive/Good/Average
3. 51st – 100th positions as Struggling or failing/Poor/Below Average

It is obvious that the teachers are either too knowledgeable for their students or the majority of the students are nincompoops.
The *"school na scam"* chant as is the title of this book, is defrauding us of talents, skills, or even gifts.

John C. Maxwell, who is one of my favorite authors points at the failings of the school system when he noted that:

- More than 50% of all CEOs of Fortune 500 companies had C or C-averages in college.

- 65% of US senators came from the bottom half of their school classes.

- More than 50% of all millionaire entrepreneurs never finished college.

What school calls "talent" is not worth a dime in the outside world; your brilliancy in Mathematics, Government, English, Biology, or what have you is not worth a thing. I have nothing to prove but it is important that I quickly let you know; I didn't do poorly in school, but I soon realized that once I got out of school, doing poorly or greatly in school might not determine – will not ever determine my level of wealth.

I hope for sure that at the very end of these few flips of pages, you will be one of those who believe school is not a scam; but its methods are! You will understand that formal education is good but not your life's-determinant for success and most importantly; you will know that your worth is not determined by your grades.

**NOTE: Education is not limited to the four walls of the classroom, most people only read to pass (Garbage in and out). More so, we do not acquire knowledge; thereby rendering our certificates useless.**

# Chapter 1

## I WANT TO BE A DOCTOR
### Choosing a career path

*"When a man has put a limit on what he will do; he has put a limit on what he can do"*

-Charles Schwab

The saying "setting your mind to do something" would have been good; if that 'something' will not cost you the experience you might have had from trying out other things.

When I was ten, it was the close of the twentieth Century; I had just completed my common entrance (that is, the First School Leaving Certificate Examination). I observed that most of those who lived very 'comfortable' lives were career people. The truth is, I didn't observe this; I had been spoon-fed into believing that those who were career people are rich, comfortable, and happy. The society where I had grown up made it seem like those who are Doctors, Lawyers, Engineers, or Civil Servants as the case may be are the 'happy' ones.

In school, a song trended and could still be in vogue for schools; the song says: "the schooled will wear shiny, pointy and classy shoes; while the unschooled (illiterate or drop out) will wear slides, tattered and not-so presentable ones". It didn't dawn on me that this wasn't just a scam; this was one of the biggest lies I have ever heard.

Whenever I was asked about my career choice, being a doctor comes to mind. Many of my friends wanted to be lawyers; some others were engineers and the very ambitious ones want to be presidents of the nation. Today, I can't figure out where those friends of mine are but I know for sure that I am not a doctor; in fact, I was never close to being a doctor, and won't -most likely- ever become a doctor.

The school then helped me to think that being a good pupil will aid me in becoming a good student; this will further aid me into my undergraduate years, then I could become a full-fledged graduate with the potential to live a happy, prosperous life. Yet, it didn't happen that way; it is different in real life. I would not blame my teachers who indoctrinated this logic – or should I say 'illogic' unto us; they were just as dogmatic to the illogic as I was, only to eventually find out something had gone wrong.

My dad was not very schooled; his highest level of education must have been O-level. He did his best to make us (myself, himself, and my stepmom) comfortable; yet, I won't deny that even he, had the problems of the school entrenched in his doctrine. He was a plumber and a good one at it; he goes from state to state working on projects, and he doubles also as an estate agent which in those years was a lucrative business. All the laws that have to do with possessing multiple streams of income must have been fulfilled by this man (please that is my dad!). I only observed as I grow and ruminate about those years that he was not rich either, he was not happy – I see him laugh but not with the fulfillment of having your needs and wants to be met.

Let's not bore ourselves with another person's biography; my point, which might not be correct is that: the school system helped us to choose a path, learn a trade, want a career, and become a good member of staff; but the school never taught us about the evolving condition of the world at large. By telling us we are strong, they were creating the weak for life.

I was one of the topmost pupils of my school yet during the common entrance result ranking, I didn't rank top 100 in the state, which means I might not even rank up to the first 3000 in the nation. Now let us see the big picture, within the small confine that my school has; I was amongst those called 'excellent'; while cutting through the state, in the ranking, I will be amongst those called 'average or good'; yet, if we go as far as the nation, I might never have ranked up to below average; I might just be amongst those deemed 'poor'.

I started as a multitalented little child, but wanted to be a doctor since the career path was made to be deemed prestigious – it is prestigious. Many others chose a career path because their family tradition allows such; some chose their career path to complement what is lacking in their family. Most of us young chaps never chose our career path because of our guts, innate ability, or even God's will for our lives; and the school helped us to continue treading this destructive path.

Many students chose to offer engineering at the undergraduate level just because somewhere along the line, they had memorized the principle of calculus and basic trigonometry; ask them what problem they are out to solve and they may never see any. Some others want to become lawyers because their literature teacher who studied law but could not practice has attested to their literature memorization skills. We can't keep recycling our failed logic and expect that the country's economy will get better. It definitely won't!

Charles Schwab's statement now applies, because of the lid of first, second, third, and others that the school placed on many of us during our tender years, we want to be first at something, and not great at many things. We all want to be called 'successful' without having to make mistakes, we all put a limit on our learning so we would not be deemed stupid at what we do not know.

Many moved to the arts during their senior secondary school days because their teachers in JSS told them that they cannot cope with either pure science or social science. Some others chose sciences because they do not want to be classed amongst the weak ones – that is so me!

In choosing a career path, we should never choose what is trendy, what is lucrative, or what has been chosen for us; I would rather advise that you choose where you can learn the most, fail the most, and still have fun the most. I am not a fan of trial and error, but I think absolutely that those who succeed a lot at things are those who have failed a lot at those things.

A typical example is the man Abraham Lincoln (if I was him, I might have quit) his political career was more of a failure story than it was a success story. He kept on failing higher and forward; never stopped failing, not shy of being termed a failure; we all know how it ended.

Albert Einstein was termed unteachable, yet he must have had the credit of being one of the greatest scientists who ever lived. Don't forget we are talking about education here, and not the gatherings of certificates; and education is about making a whole lot of mistakes, asking questions, and still learning as you go.

We most of the time come out of school unprepared for the worst-case scenario; the way our minds have been fine-tuned is such that we have a 'get-out-of-poverty' free card on our certificates. Yet, that never is the case.

To make money, the kind of money for exchange; and I mean legitimately, we need to set our school certificates aside and use our in-born certificates – our guts, mind, and brains.

In whatever field or career, we tread, we must surely know that doing it the same way as it had always been will mean that we will soon plateau, and very much become quickly away from relevance. We do need to create new ways for things to be done. I am not sorry to accuse the school of not teaching this, I could only be sorry that it seems too late for too many to learn this; Is it?

*"Although he was a son, he learned obedience through what he suffered"*
-Hebrews 5:8 RSV

You might think of me as wrong but learning is not the same as memorizing; it is experiencing, it is practical; it is trying and sometimes failing.

# Chapter 2

## BUT I USED TO ASK QUESTIONS
### *That's rebellion!*

*"Many people know the outcome of an event, only a few know the why's. A lot others don't even care"*
                              -Anonymous

One very special gift given to humans (at birth) is the innate ability to ask questions; Questions like WHY, WHAT, HOW, WHICH, WHEN, and WHERE are the basis behind every human discovery. Every invention came from inquisitiveness. The school has helped a lot of people to learn not to ask questions and because we have learned for years, how not to ask questions, we become very uncreative, unskillful, and without courage.

When we were at the very tender years – say around 1 to 3 years old, we were allowed to ask questions; we were allowed to spoil things, and we were allowed to be stupid enough to try things out. During this period of our lives, our innate inquisitiveness was alive, flourishing, and glowing; due to this, our creativity flourished as well. But as we began to 'age' a bit more, restrictions came to how many questions we could ask. All our questions came under filters, it became a crime to be stupid and we began to chicken out. Our brevity became lost – and for those whose brevity was not lost, it was there but was given no voice.

'I might get knocked', 'I might be mocked', 'this question might be stupid'; those became the new things we could create, instead of finding out how. Instead of being able to create solutions due to the new knowledge our questions will help us to acquire, we are only able to go as far as creating excuses. It is always one excuse after the other, one reason to not ask a question or the other. They told us life is 'simpler' without those questions, but they made life —our lives— harder.

In the basic classes, teachers would ask "if we understand the subject matter". On responding with a no, he would give instructions to ask any question; only that there is an undertone of judgment in his instruction, he has already judged us as either stupid or unteachable; either a dummy or a below-average pupil.

It got more complicated during the days of JSS & SSS; because now we do not raise our voices to ask a question that seems to contradict or object to the teacher's methodology. We don't ask questions that make us look 'uncool' amidst our mates, our colleagues – who are students like us; have also grown in such an environment and they have earned a new paradigm that says "Even in the subtlest situations, questions make you look stupid.

During the year 2005, I was definitely in SS2; we had a very beautiful and intelligent Biology teacher. She was a corps member and we all knew that she was very good at Biology. She knew how to name every organism – maybe not all; botanically. She could explain the then 'Modern Biology' textbook from front to back page without having to open the textbook. She knew all the topics and subtopics; we all were wowed by her depth of knowledge. One flaw that she seemed to have was that she would rather have you copy notes than discuss them with us. Her notes were bulky, let me put it in context, it was almost like copying the 'Modern Biology' text verbatim. Many of us objected, yet we were termed rebels; we were well punished and eventually, we began to avoid her class; one for one. I was always noting the timetable just so I could find a way to cut Biology class.

As if this was not enough, we had another teacher who taught us Mathematics; she was even better than the former, yet her problem was never wanting to be 'drawn backward'; she did not like you asking her questions that seemed to take a chunk out of her time. It was always painful to us as we couldn't grasp as much as we wanted. We were limited to the interest of this teacher; 'the syllabus must be covered' and asking questions or answering them might cause a delay which in turn will cause us to be unable to cover 'the syllabus'.

Here goes the real issue, the teacher must have learned in the training college, that, not covering the syllabus makes you less than your colleagues. Schools must have been told that teachers who do not cover syllabuses are incompetent. Educational inspectors must have been guided by a principle- syllabus or nothing, and that is why when teachers who were not even interested in teaching get the rumor of a visiting inspector, they quickly rush into covering the syllabus. As if this complication is not enough, our homes and society even make it worse. Parents give instructions just for their children to follow; these instructions have no whys, ifs, if nots, and hows; just follow! It is like telling a farmer that a single corn seed sown should reap two hundred maize combs; no ifs or if nots.

The 'evil' committed by our educational system cannot be blamed on the acrimony of the same system towards people; it rather should be blamed on the subtlety of our level of ignorance across society. A creative child who had unlimited potential grows up to become a dormant robot following the instructions of garbage – in and out. Nine out of ten adults only want to follow instructions; they are less responsible because we have taught them so to be. We have given them a reason to believe that life has no cost or effect provided you are not creative. Meanwhile, what we (the educational system) do to them is, make them people without grit, without effrontery.

Let's assume that Adam had been told the names of animals, birds, plants, insects, and other creatures; then, I would have blamed this 'No question asked' mentality on God. But because of God's nature of creativity; he brought them all before Adam and gave him the chance to use his initiative and creativity to take responsibility. He gave Adam a plain paper and his assignment to Adam was *"create whatever name you deem fit"* (Gen. 2:19).

Our educational system only wants the hidden answer – and when I say hidden answer; I meant the one they had written down in their mark book. They don't want you to create your answer. One very obvious example is the simple Math 1+1; if one is added to one, the answer is expected to be two; most times this is correct, but not always. What if the 1 was one-half? What if the student was thinking in terms of marriage,  where both were supposed to add up to one? What if the student read it out as one-cross-one? But the system of schools' marking always nails those who think outside their not-too-wide box as either foolish or rebellious.

My assumed solution is to allow for more questions and to be more open. What I think of an ideal situation, an ideal classroom where real learning takes place is a place where you can be a fool, full of mistakes and you won't be scared of folly. It should be a place of acceptance and help; not a place of hatred, stigmatization, or even pity.

*"Those who ask questions on a matter, are interested in its reasons"*
                    -A native saying

NOTE: My philosophy might not be the most acceptable; it might even be less formal or seem too inconsistent. It is just that what we call consistency in the school is not consistency; It is gradually becoming STEREOTYPE, STAGNANT, and helping our APATHY. Let's ask more whys, hows, wheres, and whens...it will make this world better!

# Chapter 3

## WHO SAID JEZEBEL WAS EVIL?
### *Delilah was a Demon; Sarah was a Saint*

*"No problem can withstand the assault of sustained thinking"*
                    -John C. Maxwell

A young Philistine lady was given the task to lure her lover into the snare of his enemy. The young lady had fallen in love with a Hebrew champion and their love was sure to blossom, but the cultural and geographical difference brings them looming darkness. The young man, in question, had defended his hometown (Israel) from the rulers and powers of the Philistines.

Despite warnings from his parents and families, he chose above everyone else, this beautiful young Philistine lady. Knowing fully well that his love for their descent (the lady) was true, the Philistine elders and warriors began to threaten the lady's relatives; making sure she comes under more pressure. Not the best way I would like to end this story, but the lady (Delilah) yielded to the pressure and ensnared her lover by getting the secret of his power; she gave him what was forbidden and he became powerless. The Philistine elders held Samson captive, got him blinded, and tortured him. A lot more happened but this book might not delve into that.

Just as the Philistine elders used punishment, neglect, and isolation as a means to motivate Delilah; the school system motivates us into 'learning' by that. What they call motivation tactics is not, it is subjecting us to fear. The best gift the school system seems to have given us is the right and wrong mentality – one must be right and others must be wrong.

Another gift given to us by the school system is not gender inequality as many will call it, they have given us social and mental bias. Delilah, if asked about what she did to Samson, must have her reasons. Her parents were threatened, her hometown was under siege, and her future was under question; since everyone seeks security, she wanted to earn it – at least for her people.

The current world, the society, and most importantly; the education system, puts a lot of pressure on us. It seems like the system tells us that "until Samson – that is our colleague who seems to be doing better - is brought down, you can't climb higher". The system makes many talented people suffer torment at the hands of rejection and belittling them. Others who would see, and have an eye for strange ideas that could have changed the world have been made blind; they have been shut down and subjected to recycling junks and memorization.

The school has unwittingly- may be intentionally; taught us to love mediocrity, go with the flow and never conflict with the norm. The school has kind of told us, 'don't go to Philistia to marry' – they have told us the best way to live is not to make mistakes.
I will not go on nailing everything on the school, because like Delilah, we were also stupid enough to follow the school's flow. The mirage painted for us has grown to become an image and a god we now serve; our logic came from the illogic the school sold to us, we gullibly bought into it, we love it, we don't want to unlearn it; and even if we do get the chance to do otherwise, we want to stick to the easy. We are looking everywhere for a shortcut and the school has helped us.

The school has told us, "work hard, get good grades, get a good job, work hard, earn your paycheck; and life would be easier". We failed to do otherwise, we failed to tell our financial 'Samson' that trouble is looming.

We brought our wealth into bondage because we wanted the security that is not secure.

Just so you know, Delilah, Samson, and a great number of Philistines perished at the very end of that story. In the same vein, we, the school system, and the society at large comes under siege of poverty and face the peril of financial decadence. How did we get here? We ask, but we never would think better even if we found out since we already have a paradigm we love and never want to quit.

UNLIKE Delilah, society did not force Jezebel, right? Well, I don't know. All I know is Jezebel had her whys too. She had an irresponsible husband, one who would not take responsibility for his wrongs. When anything goes wrong, he comes to Jezebel; who he had not invested in to take responsibility. Most times, Jezebel protected what was most important to her – her husband and her god. She quickly builds a wall of defense, not minding who would be hurt. Isn't that what most wise people do today? They quickly prove themselves right and every other person wrong.

Because of the school's grading system, the ones who are called brilliant, intelligent, or even geniuses do everything in their power to break the dulls' ego. Even the teacher helps to make this happen, like Jezebel; our 'brilliant' students are helped by the policymakers, the school administrators, and the class teachers to feel that everything they have memorized (let me say learned) – is all that is ever important and that those who can't learn memorization are their feeble opponents, and are meant to be trodden upon. It now brings us back to the war front we have wanted to avoid – and we could; the war of right and wrong.

The school, which was said to be the second and one of the most important agents of socialization, therefore, becomes the best

agent of division. The school now has a divide and rule principle; either a technique of teacher against students or the 'smart' students against the 'dull' ones.
Learning is beyond what you 'know'. I said 'know' because what school calls knowledge is a list of facts crammed; a list of right answers to a list of questions.

Robert Kiyosaki gave one of the best examples I have seen to describe learning. He used the bicycle and treadmill logic to describe what school does to us (though I don't blame it on the school). He said if they ask us about models of bicycles, materials for making bicycles, when bicycles were invented, how many tires a bicycle possesses, or who invented the bicycle; the highest practical form of learning we could get from the school is trying to pedal with a stationary treadmill.

Most people learn cognitively but the affective and psychomotor aspect is lost. No wonder there is a tendency for a higher percentage of failures in the real world, where all these domains of learning come to play. If I truly want to learn to ride a bicycle, I don't particularly need to know; who, when, or how the bicycle was made; I might not even know what material makes up the bicycle. What I truly need is to attempt and keep attempting to ride a bicycle with an instructor – a guide, helping me in my course.

The school teaches us to not fall off the bicycle, so they give us the treadmill, where we do not have to be mobile; all we have to do is pedal and sweat on a spot. The school tells us to work hard – at least at the things they think are right; don't make mistakes, don't fall off, and never ask for help. They tell us we don't need a team when they give us class work and examinations, but they use a team when they try to explain to us. This is one of the most contradicting systems I have seen.

Let us quickly return to Jezebel; she protected what was most important to her but detrimental; that is, at the detriment of the nation, her husband, her lineage, and at the cost of her life. If there be any positive I ever saw in Jezebel, it would be that at least, she was ready to live and die for what she believed was right. Only that, what she believed was right, was not, in reality.

Many of us live this kind of life too; we have been spoon-fed into believing a falsehood. The "get a good job with good pay and more benefits" has become a mantra we want to live and die for; but we do not hold dear the most important essence of school which is: to learn; to make mistakes; not ever cover up; to be flawed but grow; to know how to have real essence without having to diminish others; to earn wealth that is lasting and not just money; to see from other people's standpoint and not only ours; to seek correct security — in the really important things and not in that which fades; to pursue not a mirage, but a true image; to make friends and build relationships; to know people's weaknesses but never exploit them; to reach for the best, both for ourselves and many others. This is education – the best legacy.

*"Nobody who ever has his best regretted it"*
-George Halas

**NOTE: Do not be brainwashed! No one is entirely evil, no one is entirely a saint. Everyone has something to protect; it is just that I advise that in all of these, learning makes you see beyond the surface. It helps you see beyond others' judgment. It is meant to be a launch pad to a world of infinite possibilities. If anyone reaches the very height of good or bad, check their thinking; and if you are done, ask where they learned it**

**from. The school's role can never be overemphasized, when it comes to our thoughts; and our thoughts determine our actions. "...as a man thinketh, so is he".**

# Chapter 4

## THE REAL VILLAINS
### *School; Teacher; Policymakers; Society; Government*

*"It is not enough to do our best; sometimes we have to do what is required"*
                    - Winston Churchill

A lot of folks have done their best to improve 'education', but as much as they do, we still notice a trend of decadence, that started by making sure schooling became a vital part of our everyday life. One of the things that I have particularly noticed is that: parents nail it on teachers; teachers on educational inspectors; inspectors nail it on policy makers; policy makers nail it on the government; and eventually, the blame game gets across to the large society.

One of my favorite lecturers during my university days first taught me while I was in 200L. Her course was an elective requirement for courses I had to offer. Many of my classmates didn't want to offer the course, they said: "This woman had never taught us, she is not predictable". A close friend said: "I don't want a course that will cause my CGPA to dwindle". I also didn't know what to expect, but the time for course registration was running out, and it seemed I had limited options. So, I chose to offer her course and face whatever problem I would have headlong.

My thoughts were: "my CGPA is not bad but great; having to do poorly in this course would not cause me too much". I registered for the course expecting the 'worst' and as I expected, only six of us offered the course, and one of those six never attended classes. To my greatest surprise, our class sections were not like any other; it was a class where the lecturer spoke less and we talked more;

a class where we wrote no notes, but we enjoyed and understood so well; a class where, at the end of the semester, we all couldn't conclude topics, but we all could conclude concepts. The examination came and all six of us wrote it. After submission, five of us were able to write as much as we could, only one of us didn't have anything to record – we knew why, but that was not the point. The point was all five who participated actively in the class wrote different things, yet passed well.

Two semesters later, we had a project we were running with this lecturer so she needed to refer; she had to go to our scripts and while we were sorting things out, she confessed that the department was furious that four out of six students each had an ' A' in her course. I was alarmed, yet proud that she stood her ground. Before now, I would have blamed the department; but now I know, that even the faculty rarely produces first-class students; and the whole university produces less than three hundred (300) first-class graduates. This is a university that produces not less than nine hundred (9000) graduates per session.

I could well say that teachers to students are villains because no student wants to feel like an idiot. No man wants to feel less than important, and results when pasted make some feel less wise than they are. The teacher breaks the students' ego; why then, wouldn't he be 'hated'? As if that is not enough, even teachers hate the system; they feel they are underpaid. They feel they are treated less than their counterparts who are in other fields. They feel doing something else makes more impact on society. Oh, not to worry, it does not end there. The system – school system; blames the government.

The school system hates the government, and the whole educational system – at least in Nigeria, feels like the government is not doing enough. They feel the government is not pumping enough funds into making sure that the system runs without hassles. Well, the government of the day also has someone to blame. They go as much as to blame the immediate past administration, for leaving them a mess to repair; they blame citizens for being less patriotic, and too dependent on the government's relief and policies. The blame continues and runs on and on without succor or repair; without help or relief; without amends or stopping.

We look for the villain, but the villain is "US"; yes, US – I don't mean the United States, I mean the pronoun "US". We are the 'architects of our misfortune"; we want a tiny part of the whole, to solve the problem created by the whole. No, it doesn't work that way; to solve a problem created by all, then all is needed.

We want to increase the standard of admitting students into schools; meanwhile, that will mean we will have to term source;

'INDOMITABLE'. We want to increase the income of teachers, that's very good, but that will tell on our budget. We want to re-supervise how teachers are doing things; yet, that will mean they will work out of fear and not delight. Building more schools might be a nice idea, but do not forget that such a step will require more hands supervising and inspecting. I think privatization of the educational system is some sumptuous move; only that, are the private sectors empowered enough to handle something as large as our schools and its accompanying systems?

I am not trying to be a prophet of doom here, telling us that nothing can work. What I am rather insinuating is, that we can not solve a large problem with a minute move. We have to overturn it all; and it seems one of the best ways of doing this is to break the whole scoring, grading, and classing systems in schools. Another way is to eliminate the illogic of 'one answer is correct, while others are wrong'. When this is done, we can now look into grooming innate abilities, other than growing people; what to believe – or what not to believe.

Like my university, society thinks making success difficult to achieve means failure reigns supreme. I think once success becomes difficult to achieve, a lot of people will settle for mediocrity. I think calling those who do averagely in our tests, 'average' or 'slow learners', makes our society slower in progress. I think terming anyone, a 'poor student', less than his or her colleagues, means such a person will find interest in doing anything else – including a crime.

I think our marking scheme is only a scheme against the growth and development of our economy. We have 'killed' many colombuses before they even lift their shoes; we have capsized their ship, wreaking havoc on their team before they have ever gone assail; what an irony! Teamwork is not encouraged; not by social stratification, nor would it be encouraged by educational satisfaction; where the 'A' student can't truly do well with their lives.

I recently heard about one of my colleagues who wasn't great back then in school. She was one of those, whom I believe the educational system would term average – may be less. I learned she recently won herself an award in trading. I don't know the details of this, but unlike many of us who were praised by the school, she was failed by it. Yet, she believed that she isn't a failure (which isn't happening to many classed 'failures'). She knows that she might not be great at what we studied – or was told to study, but she is a greatly talented and skilled person. She must have followed her passion or must have been taught to try out something else. At the very least, I was happy, when I heard about her exploits in her new field.

We all have sold ourselves this lie enough; we need to quit it. We need to break this ceiling over us, we need to stop this thing we call 'education' and truly do education. We need to stop failing those who truly need the school, we need to stop killing colombuses and stop ship-wreaking them. We need to allow the next generation, to remember us for a change that caused them all, or, at least, a majority of them, to thrive and not just survive.

The blame game must stop; parents must stop telling their children to not make mistakes, and teachers must embrace mistakes and help the students see life from the light of their 'failure', and not an answer. Systems should not give teachers the effrontery to do it the 'right way' which may or may not be 'their' way. The government must first lead 'themselves' to thinking beyond the box before leading others out of the box – not into the box. Most importantly, society at large, must see mistakes as a part of our lives and not a plague that needs to be avoided.

*"Inspiration is easy; implementation is the hard part"*
-Bob Taylor

*"The reason I know so much is because I have made so many mistakes"*
-R. Buckminster Fuller

*"For I am the best...unfit...on the contrary, I worked harder than any..."*
-1 Corinthians 15:9-10

**NOTE: The blame game does not help anyone, rather, it makes everyone, including yourself, a villain. Why don't we all, like Paul, work hard at our failings? Why don't we just allow**

the Edisons of today, to keep experimenting – at least with a guise; till the results come forth?  A tiny little answer may not solve a giant problem; yet, vice versa could happen.

# Chapter 5

## FRAUD
### *At least School did not teach that!*

*"Men are alike in their promises. It is only in their deeds that they differ"*
-Molière

When I think about fraud,  the very first thing that comes to mind is the tendency I had shown toward being fraudulent. I wish I could hate on those who are, but I find it hard to hate them. I have come to realize that they just seem to not find a better way or they have been taught to not 'find' a better way. One of the influences of school on many of us is the thought pattern that seems to say, "if it works for you, then it's all good", "if you can make it, don't search for another way even if you're making it mar others".

When I was ten, we were preparing for Christmas, and most schools then used to give their pupils a promise card each. This promise card was used to raise money for the school's end-of-year and Christmas party. Though the school will surely charge all pupils a fee for the Christmas party, whatever we could gather via our cards used to serve as the extra that makes the party more beautiful. Every pupil was put under compulsion to deliver.

Truthfully speaking, it was fun; we got to connect with people outside our immediate setup because we wanted to deliver. Yet, it sponsored the spirit of competition; those who could not hit the assumed target were tagged failures. Knowing that I could hit the target, I wanted more. I wanted to make money for myself; I wanted to get my promise card to my uncles, aunts, area brothers, and sisters – and I mean my promise card.

So, I worked with a friend, a bit older than I was (he was about 13 years old). We created our promise card; but we had a limit, our promise card was not printed. We thought deep, then walked up to a business center (that is what we call a printing shop, right?). We explained a bit of our plight to them, but we told a lie knowing that the man in charge of the shop will enquire further into our promise card business. We lied to him that we were sent by the school. He agreed to every one of our terms – that to our surprise, we concluded and we fixed a date to come get our finished work.

Two days later, at school, we all were hearing the voice of tension; we automatically knew the wrath of the school was coming upon a pupil, but we didn't know who it was. I was initially not bothered until rumors spread that one of us forged the school's promise card. I knew I was in trouble but I did not mind.

Long story made short, the man we met at the business center entered my class, looked through, and pointed at me. I was summoned to the proprietor's office and was interrogated on who my accomplice was. I confessed all and was severely dealt with ( when I say severely, I meant beaten, battered, and corporally punished). I saw my dad's disappointment and how angry he was. I now understand it!

My real confession in the matter was, that I wasn't completely remorseful; although I was sad that I had disappointed my dad, and had earned myself a bad name. What made me sad was that I didn't get the opportunity to make my money.

At age ten, my real sorrow was not the tarnishing of my image; my real sorrow was having to labor without result, having to fill a promise card for my school and not myself; having to be 'betrayed' by a so-called 'partner' – the man in charge of the business center. My real sorrow wasn't about lying and being caught, my real sorrow was the failure of my money-making plan. It wasn't about the pain inflicted by the corporal punishment, it was about the pain inflicted by the lack of opportunity to fatten my account.

The essence of this story is not to play down the fraudulent tendency – lying about the promise card was fraudulent; and I never would advise any fraudulent practice – at least not again.

The school never teaches us to be fraudulent, it never teaches us to be bad; rather, it teaches each student to be a good citizen, to obey authorities, and to progress in the community. This, for me, is something the school does very well; the school does this with great finesse, excellence, and a lot of enthusiasm. The school does not teach any child to be corrupt, but we need to know that the school also fails to teach the child how not to be corrupt.

As much as we were all told to be good, to be obedient, to be disciplined, and to find dignity in labor; we seem to lack the information on how not to be bad. What do I mean? The school wants us to be acceptable citizens of our society doing the 'right' things. The 'right' things meanwhile are the things that a 'not-right' system has taught us. What I am saying in essence is; that the school didn't teach many of us how to be financially independent and free. Since human nature wants to "have and have", we fail to understand that we don't need a crooked means to get what we want. If a nine-year-old wants to make money all because he wants to feel good, what would a ninety-five-year-old man feel about making money?

Fraud – or corruption as it affects this country; is not a case of who is right or wrong. It is a matter for all of us. Acceptability is one of the most important needs of anyone, and knowing that gathering wealth will make you acceptable will mean that everyone is in pursuit of making it. Indeed, most of us do not know how to legitimately gather wealth. We conclude, most of the time, that, having money to spend is wealth; I beg to differ.

A lot of politicians have done their dues; borrowing money for campaigns, using family properties as collateral, and taking a lot of risks because they 'know' that earning a political office is a sure means of getting much more than they ever spent – lawfully or unlawfully. A lot of young men stick to their PCs, and download different pictures from the internet just to build a gallery for fraudulent practice – Yahoo na! or you no know am? Let's talk about ladies who purchase waist beads worth hundreds of thousands just to make their sexual partners their financial slaves. All these may only be common in this part of the world, yet one thing reflects as the cause, and that is the need for money.

The school didn't teach us to be fraudulent, but it failed to teach us how to make, sustain and pass on wealth legitimately. Those who even studied money in school – accountants and economists are part of those being ravaged by the worst kind of poverty. The country's economy lacks sustenance, the people live under the poverty line. Law and order are failing, and that is because 'corruption' – the normal human tendency is reigning.

I have called fraud a normal human tendency, and a lot of people might deem me incorrect. How do you explain this? A sucking child bites his mother's nipple and looks at the mother's face with a smile. The child might just be enjoying himself or having the fun of his little life, but at whose detriment? Every human – woman or man, boy or girl, aged or young, able-bodied or disabled; wants to be special, feel special, and be treated specially. We most times do not care who we hurt to have it. Only a paradigm change can make us care.

True wealth can never come by doing what is detrimental to the world around us, or anyone. True wealth is; having enough to cater for one's self, those around, and those to come, without having to harm anyone or anything emotionally, physically, spiritually, and mentally. True wealth is the process of making yourself and the world better with the money you have. True wealth can only be gotten via legal means.

Looking again at my story, the school corrected (punished) my wrong without ever encouraging or praising my 'right'. I was creative enough to think of ways to get money and was only termed guilty of plagiarizing the school's property; by forging the school's promise card. No one ever credited the depth of my thinking, all everyone did was discard all the good, due to the bad. If the school wouldn't help children to channel their wants for money, and their need for wealth creation into something useful, legal, and sustainable; we will move to have in our hands, a messier society.

Gone are the days when parents leave scraps of electronics for their children to play with; oh, how beautiful were those days! Now, all we do is spoon-feed the next generation with the information we deem important. We discard anything else, even the innate inquisitiveness of a child. No wonder society seems deformed.

*"While your circumstances are beyond your control; your character is not"*
           - John C Maxwell

It is important that I also say this to the larger society; even though our circumstances might be demining or undermining, and our backgrounds might not be encouraging; how we react, how we tread, and how we do things are solely based on our thought pattern. We can not always blame the school system for failing us, because, we also fail ourselves. We forget that one's entire life is a tiny drop that is surrounded by countless tiny drops. Yet, that tiny drop (life) can affect other drops drastically.

*"CHARACTER is the sum of our everyday choices"*
> \- Margaret Jensen

*"Wealth brings money, never friends..."*
> -Proverbs 19:4 (RSV)

*"A good name is to be chosen rather than riches..."*
> -Proverbs 22:1 (RSV)

**NOTE:** All fraudulent activities, no matter how subtle, are not created by the school's failure to teach us about wealth creation. They are most times created by human-presumed needs to be top and special. The school has the responsibility to teach us to better our minds and habits, not just to better our positions. We have the right to make choices, so why not make the right ones?

# Chapter 6

## THE EARLY MEN
### *Financial Intelligence?*

*"No sparrow surpasses another, only the ones who have climbed the ridge"*
                    - Native Yoruba Adage

The rate at which our society (our age) condemns the culture of the early men is alarming. I think we see them as unlearned, savage, cannibalistic, and primitive. This could be very true, it is just that we are worse than they are; we think we are learned, we think we are wise, but many of us are as primitive as they are. Many of us are not consuming humans, we are not offering human sacrifices – at least. However, we have proven to ourselves that they seem better off. During their time, the word 'corruption' had not been invented;

during their age, everyone had something to give or offer.

Permit me to bring it to our black society, since I am black. We nail our forefathers who lived before and during the colonial era for being gullible. We think of them as lacking enlightenment, at least if they did, they would not sell their sons, daughters, lands, and raw materials for mirrors (maybe that is what we were told). Unlike them, we are enlightened; we have been to the four walls of the classroom, we have social media, we have a government of our own, and laws that bind us. We think of ourselves as superior beings; people with a higher level of understanding, in an age that is well-groomed, nurtured by civilization and aided by technology.

The only limitation is; that we didn't learn from their mistakes. The early men or our forefathers had their very many flaws which are very obvious to our age. They are conspicuously visible for us to see; compared to their flaws, we could call ourselves infallible only to fall even shorter than they did.

The early men were men without 'clothes'; lacking in technology, they never had a formal education system, and the government was not as generalized as it is now. It was mostly every man for himself, every tribe with its leader, every family with its head. The tribes were most of the time, unable to inter-trade due to language barriers. They lived in what we call 'abject poverty'; from hand to mouth daily. Professionalism was 'simple'; it was farming, fishing, and hunting. Entertainment came at work or in the house, and work was much more 'tedious' than we have it now. They did not have a lot to point at, no development to chase after, they were living as much as their mouths could feed.

Let me not forget to talk about conflict and resolution of the same; wars were fought via physical contact, there were no guns, bullets, bombs, viruses, or cyber-attack. Yet, they found a way to thrive. At least the powerful held onto their powers while the less powerful fed on to stay alive.

One very important practice in their days was barter – yes, I mean "trade by barter". There wasn't a uniform currency and everyone traded with what they had - money, grains, tubers, lands, or cowries. No one wanted to possess just one thing; they all (okay, maybe not all of them) wanted to have what they had not, with much readiness to give up what they had. To them, money was about exchange and not about possessions or amounts of credit alerts.

They made women who could multitask, to control the real roots of economic growth such as farming, shelter, trade (though, not in all cases), family, and other aspects.

Women (including children), were most of the time declared labor-free. Men stayed at the helm of security and public affairs. Life was simple and "simplicity was beauty", at least for them. They were uncivilized, unschooled, yet, full of wisdom. The ratio of those who were professionally and financially secure greatly outweighs the not secure ones; this term to them never existed, but it is what it is.

Here comes our age, where we threw to thrash all the great works they had done and blame them for the one thing that led to the loss of their independence and security – GREED. We lash at them; meanwhile, many of those who came to a generation before us became 'rich' through real estate and agro-investment (something many of the ancient guys willed unto us).

The early men or at least those who lived during or before the colonial era didn't lose their freedom to the western world because they were unlearned, rather, they lost their freedom when they became selfish- a religion the western world sold to them. Like Dale Carnegie puts that concept, "the western world arouses in the other person, a need, a desire".

Due to this longing, our forefathers began to let go of their sons, daughters, brothers, and even sisters, for the things they had never seen. They lost 'real security' for security (a mirage that wouldn't ever be real). I think the colonial masters had fought their way through, but they wouldn't win. I think they had lost grounds to these "unlearned men", that they became wiser (and I do not mean the winning black men, I meant the losing colonial masters.

They inadvertently found out that they couldn't win by siege means but they could by guile. Our forefathers were beguiled into thinking that security was teaming up with their opponents against their teammates.

They began to let go of farming, cloth making, barter trading, and a lot more. Just so you know, the colonial masters subscribed to barter; they saw this from the 'ignorant' men's angle and that brought them dominance. They knew we were religious, they gave religion to us; they knew we loved good things, they offered them to us; they knew we were power-driven, and they willingly called us to power – but at what cost?

I might have had my biases, so I leave you to be the judge; but what I am saying, is that the early men who never visited the walls of the classroom understood "financial intelligence" and "financial security". They were not after possessions, rather, they were after assets; anytime they had something beyond their need, they termed it as a liability and traded such for 'assets'.

Another very wise thing they did was invest. They never ate the best tuber from each year's harvest, they rather sowed it. They believed sowing the best always brings a better harvest, and it always worked, pests and diseases notwithstanding. The real failure they were unable to correct was their greed; it led them to take liabilities from their 'enemy'- the colonial masters. They unwittingly traded off their assets for a piece of bread!  It is true that our colonial masters brought us globalization, but are we the ones globally influential or them? – Oh, my bias again!

The school is gradually recycling their mistakes into the curriculum; 'one way is right, tread it or be wrong'. Meanwhile, those men we called unlearned, ignorant, and primitive understood that many paths can be right; staking your life and skill on only one path means you are 'doomed' to un-satisfaction, discontent, and most likely regret. Farmers planted in those days, not knowing what will happen to the seed sown. They went to the market to barter, not knowing who would bring what they needed or from what culture he would stem. Yet, they made more anyway.

The school taught us to do our best and plan our lives on a path; the path of "I am right, others are wrong". They told us to pass the exams, graduate as one of the best (if not the best), get a good job, and be secure. Yet, what they call 'security' is the reprogramming of the mistakes of our forefathers.

I truly hope the future generation will not meet the mess we have made; I hope they won't call us primitive and unlearned, despite our array of degrees. I hope we won't teach them to hate the 'former way' just to seek new security. I hope they won't inherit the "you are wrong" mentality. I hope when they look back at this part of the 21st Century, they will call us the groundbreakers, true change makers, and not the ones who brought poverty. I also do not think that any school teaches us wealth as it is used for exchange, I do not think any school makes us see that money has wings.

I hope we would know that an accumulation of credentials doesn't make you – a sparrow, taller than the other; it is just a privilege you have in climbing the ridge. When the ridge is gone (with accumulated liabilities), you will return to your heights. I hope we will know that wealth is not only financial; it is also spiritual, emotional, mental, physical, medical, and psychological. I hope we know, I hope we do!

*"Wealth hastily gotten will dwindle, but he who gathers little by little will increase it"*
-King Solomon (of Ancient Israel)
Around 2800 BC

 Our forefathers never went to see the four walls of the classroom; they were uncivilized. Some of the greatest scientists failed woefully with the classroom 'box'. Many of them learned to read and write by themselves. Do I hate school? I've never done it! What I hate are the lies that society has helped us to believe. What I hate is that the school, which is supposed to take the scales off our faces, has been doing great at further blindfolding us. What I hate is that the agrarian generation seems to have the advantage of practical, learner-centered learning than we of a civilized generation. What I hate the most of all, is that we go to school, yet, we have no financial education.

**Chapter 7**

## WE TEACH THEM ABOUT GOD
*Religious Organizations, Another scam?*


*"Be not righteous overmuch, and do not make yourself overwise; why should you destroy yourself?"*
-King Solomon (Around 2500 BC)
Ecclesiastes 17:6


The school and the system employed by it have failed us – not just in grades, but also in terms of the 'junks' they taught us.
Even the 'knowledge' acquired is seeming obsolete, archaic, out of date, and decayed. It is not that the school has not done well to help our enlightenment ( at least for some things), yet, it always seems like the more formal education is attained, the more difficult it is for wealth to be attained.

I am not talking in terms of money, I am rather talking about wealth in all its possible forms.

It is very tragic that; the thing appreciated by Nigerians – okay Africans, fails us much more. Our belief, culture, and dependence on a deity is seeming to fail us too. Please, I am not an atheist; at least they have their point of view and their whys. Yet, as a person who was born into a religious culture, groomed by a religious society, and has had a fair share of the practice of religion, I have seen the fallibility of religion. Yes, I mean the more religion failed to teach us about wealth creation, sustenance, and handing over.

In my own country, there is a practice of three popular religions. These three point at one thing or they assume they point at one thing; that is GOD. These religions are Christianity, Islam, and Traditional / Ancient African Religion.

## Christian Religion

Before I go on here, I would like you to know that I was born in the church and that I've gone to the church than I have attended the places of worship of other religions. My dwelling on this subject is not out of bias or hatred, it is just so I would be practical enough.

Christian teachers believe so much in God as was revealed, and is revealed through Jesus – the Christ. They believe that God gives wealth, yet in this singleness of belief are many denominations. Each denomination believes that its mode and structure; doctrine or teaching is the only true one. If any other denomination comes with a doctrine opposing to theirs, or not the same as theirs; then sabotage, enmity, or worse begins.

The leaders teach their members (not all of the leaders though) to believe in them, be mentored by them, know their pattern, and follow the same. They indoctrinate their members into believing truths they have not practiced. They tell members about a 'God' they might not have met; judgment and declaration of the course of the future events become the vogue and members gullibly follow them. I do not blame them; neither do I nail their members.

I know for sure that this 'truth' they have come to believe came from falsehood; and if there truly be a God who created the heavens and the earth, came as a man just to redeem man from sin, died to make man live and rose to give man victory; He wouldn't support falsehood.

I think that, like the words of Jesus whom they preach, what they do isn't the worship of God, but the passing on of the doctrine of men.

*"And well did Isaiah prophesy... these people honor me with their lips...teaching as precepts the doctrine of me...you love the commandment of God..."*
-Mark 7:7

## Islam

I am not a Muslim, but I practiced Islam for a few years. I have Muslim maternal grandparents, so I know how they practice. I attended Quran classes and I can quote some Arabic chapters, even if I can't say their meanings. So, when I say a thing that seems out of context, you can help me put it right.

Unlike their Christian counterparts, the leaders here do not stand under the guise of love; rather, they want you to understand the rule of conflict without mincing words.

They are not afraid to be deemed violent, provided they are defending their truth.

The Quran that came from Allah (isn't that God!), is the true foundation of all that they do – so they say. Well, I have observed that leaders here (though not all) only stand under the guise of following the Quran to the latter; meanwhile, what they do is stylishly enslave their followers. They may not request offerings and tithes, but their followers are told to gullibly hate anyone who doesn't practice what they practice (including family members). It comes easy for them to condemn, with hell, being the biggest threat that is posed. If this was all, I might not be able to say a thing; but the fact that they use FEAR TACTICS – which the school seems to use is disgusting to me. Fear has its place; yet, in perfect love (which God shows) fear is not a part. Even the great prophet (SAW) would not approve of hate.

# African Traditional Religion (ATR)

This is more diversified than I can talk about; so pardon my lack of depth in all the aspects, permit me to generalize. These seem to be the least acceptable in our 'modern' world. They seem to have quickly gone into extinction, but they haven't, they are very much here. The other religions seem to have great proof of modernization and globalization; and I would have just concluded that it was formal education that affected them so badly; but ATR, which was born from our very own culture and bred by our ancestors, also has the problem of the school.

Herbalists, native doctors, and priests/priestesses are in most cases worse than their counterparts. While some are better off, they know that there are deities of both good and evil; even the rate of their practices would rather have the good and not the evil. Yet, those who are supposed to teach this cultural religious practice to us are eviler than the devil himself.

Those who are deified were men who had to die in strange ways; defending culture, people, places, lands, and much more. Yet, our priestesses and priests only practice this religion for show and their pockets' sake. Even Esu (Satan) does the same, they claim to detest him, but they do his works. I do not understand where these lies were birthed from, but we have allowed them to grow into adulthood, and they're now uneasy to curb.

**The Man's View**

Religion has not helped us, you can agree and you have the right to disagree. I am not asking us to abolish worship unto God, I am asking us to abolish limiting and limited doctrines of men. I am asking us to break the walls that break us asunder.

I still attend church, I love the LORD, I am a Christian, and I am not shy about it;  yet, I won't hate you for whatever you practice. I do not ever like the fact that we use religion as a means of a divide amongst us.

If truly CHRIST taught to love and GOD is love; if truly JIHAD means strife to do what is good (not with another but strife within one's self). If the deities hate the devil for his cunningness (I mean Esu) and evil ways; then who do we deceive with our lies? Whose fault will it be that the societal decadence and high rate of poverty are caused by our lack of openness?
Which demon would we claim to have bewitched us if we teach hatred and limitedness? Who shall we blame if the future is oblique and unclear because we couldn't work together based on religion? I leave you to answer these questions.

*"Religion spoils everything, even Governments"*
-A driver I met today (18th March 2022)

*"Every man is fully satisfied that there is such a thing as truth, or he would not ask any question"*
- Charles Sanders Pierce (1951)

**NOTE: I don't see a why for 'religion'; I do not hate religious people, and I love those who gullibly follow religious leaders. My take is; if it is truly GOD, ALLAH, or the DEITY we are trying to promote; we wouldn't promote division. HE encourages peaceful co-existence; and when I talk about religion, I do not only mean a mode of worship, I mean faithfulness to one way of thinking – now you get it, right?**

# Chapter 8

## FOLLOW THE STATS
### *Sports' Leaderboard*

*"If he wasn't good at defending, he wouldn't be a Liverpool player"*
-Jurgen Klopp

Life in general offers us both the choice to fail and succeed. Every single day, we wake up to that chance, every breath taken points at either failing or succeeding; every activity does too. Unlike those who are deemed successful, the ones many think unsuccessful might be racking up stats for a bigger purpose. They might be doing 'unnoticeable' things, they may be 'unpopular' but everyone is going for something.

In the world of sports, the line between success and failure is so glaring; that even the blind can see it. Year in, year out; sportsmen and sportswomen compete for trophies, silverware, and some bragging rights. Social media has helped to make even the most minute things they do visible to the world.

One of the groups of sportsmen in this era is Liverpool FC. This football club is rich in history and it possesses beautiful tradition, that is, the fan and club relationship. They have had their fair share of great moments which has amounted to silverwares and lots more. The club has had a lot of legends and they have racked up stats that a lot of newbies want to break, yet it seems like the school system has also eaten deep into the rating system in the world of sports.

Names like Gerrard, Dalglish, Suarez, Torres, Salah, Mane, TAA are household names for Liverpool fans; but some others have labored tooth and nail, and worked their socks out to make sure those other names are mentioned. I will only cite two examples here.

There is a guy called Jordan Henderson; at the time of penning this, he is Liverpool's captain and it seems like that is the only reason why he is known, but many people do not know that beyond the leadership skill possessed by Henderson, he gives Liverpool FC a lot more.

In 2014, Liverpool FC lost the league to Manchester City; the team lost a game against Chelsea and drew against Crystal Palace. In both matches, Henderson was injured, which meant that he didn't feature in any of those matches. He wasn't deemed important, as the team had Steven Gerrard, Luis Suarez, Daniel Sturridge, and Raheem Sterling; these players were giving them the attacking flare.

A lot of people blamed that season's misfortune on the tragic slip of Gerrard against Chelsea; and the shambolic defending that made Crystal Palace come back to draw from 3-0 down, I don't!

Henderson was Liverpool's most potent mid-fielder. When it comes to shielding, he was always helping in breaking the opposition's attack. I assumed if Henderson had played against Chelsea, Liverpool might have drawn; and they wouldn't focus only on attacking when facing Crystal Palace.

In 2019, Liverpool again lost the league to Manchester City; this time, it was with a lot of points, but their 97 points were not enough. At the turn of January 2019, Liverpool was a table topper; the club had 7 points gap and their closest rival had only a game in hand and an Etihad ('man city' stadium) showdown against Liverpool. Well, if Manchester City had won both, Liverpool would still be leading by a point provided they won all their matches. But that January was catastrophic, the club won only one of six matches (4 in the league). Manchester City won the league again, with a 2-point gap. Long story made short, Henderson was injured against city so he couldn't play the rest of the matches in January – I hope you notice the trend.

In a game against Barcelona in May 2019, Liverpool lost the first leg; 3 goals to nothing, and Henderson didn't play. I know you must have grabbed that. All Liverpool stars featured, yet, they lost (the stars included an in-form; Mo Salah, Sadio Mane, and Roberto Formino, the worst threatening front-thrice at the time). Here comes the second leg, Liverpool completed one of the most difficult comebacks of the champion league history. Two of their superstar forwards weren't even present, they won 4-nil. Henderson made assistance for the first and was pivotal in defending against Barcelona's attack.

A year later, despite the COVID-19 global pandemic; Liverpool FC won the Premier League. Henderson again proved himself pivotal; the only match they lost before being declared league winners was against Watford and like always, he didn't play. He eventually got the recognition he deserved by winning player of the tournament. Yet, he had to wait 'seven painful' years before the world of sport saw him as pivotal to Liverpool's success.

In today's classroom, there are many Jordan Hendersons who work their socks out for the unity, progress, and peace of the class; but they are not recognized since they aren't the class toppers that is, the ones who score 'As'.

There was a girl I taught in a school for only eight months. Even though she is not the 'brightest' in her class, the class surely misses her whenever she is absent. Her classmates call her 'ATM' because no one can ever be hungry when she's around (provided she hadn't spent her all in catering for other classmates). That wasn't all, she was a good sports lady too. During inter-class football matches, even the male students do not dare to face her in goal as she is good at goalkeeping. That girl seemed to have 'resigned to destiny'; many teachers have called her dull, and not bright until she met some teachers who saw potential in her.

Well, most of us who taught her then did not last a year in the school; she might have reverted to not believing in herself. This would not be the teachers' fault, nor would it be the fault of the students. I wouldn't like to blame it on the government, I would rather not blame anyone. The system we all are following after; the system we are all pushing, and the system we all have employed seem to be failing us.

It is really easy for us to rate the smart ones and 'separate' the dull ones. But we fail to see that what we call 'smart' may never be truly smart, and those we deem 'dull' may as well be the brightest. The school system does not honor collective efforts, it rather wants all students to compete against themselves – What a pity!

Indeed, the world of sports may not reward everyone as equal as it should – that I do not like too. But the world of sports rewards both individual and collective efforts; that is why even fringe players get medals if their team ever wins a thing. Only a player can be the best in the world, but even the 'worst' of all players on winning teams get medals.
This is what I am insinuating; stats are for sportsmen, supporters, and voters; the school should not sift our innocent children based on stats; the pass against the fail, the bright against the dull; the quick learners against the slow. This is absurd!

*"To move the world, we must first move ourselves"*

-Socrates

Grading systems should have been based on character; ability to relate, ability to create (creativity), ability to question the norms, ability to think without a box, ability to function well with others; ability to lead and to follow, ability to give help when it is needed, natural tendencies; and not based on "academic prowess". It helps no one!

This thing we call 'academic prowess' might just be us using our degraded, degenerate and dissuading paradigms. We hail those who pass the exams we set, we isolate those who have the grit and cleverness to attempt, knowing that we would fail them. It would have been good if our teachers didn't cram their lecture notes by rote if they didn't set exams based on the logic of one right answer; wouldn't it be wonderful if every student sees that the teacher is not an authority that sifts them, but a mentor that guides them. Through the fingers in one hand, I could count teachers I can still call mentors today. They all have taught me, but many of them pitted me against myself at my first encounter with them.

Another very important player in the current Liverpool squad (as at the time this is penned) is Trent Alexander Arnold. He is a right full-back, young and talented; most pundits, fans, colleagues, and even opponents only hail him for his attacking ability (that is where he racks up the stats). I don't think I have seen anyone hail him for being good at his real job – defending.

A lot of analysts have hailed him, they would say it is easy to dribble past him, he is not composed when making tackles, and so on. Yet, his coach never changes his position – at least his club coach. Anytime he is not playing the right side of Liverpool, the attack is most likely dull; the most tragic part is that the same right side is vulnerable in his absence. I would beg to say that he is not defensively good, but his attacking prowess gives the team an advantage in not having to defend from that side. Most Liverpool opponents keep their left side tight, they don't even want to attack from there, they know if they do, they might be hit hard on the break and that is all. Thanks to the passing ability of this young man.

Since we are not talking sports, I will leave you to do the math. We are talking about schooling and money, and it seems the school system and the school programs do not see the relationship between success and money. Most of the time, the four walls of our classrooms teach us to be stereotyped, selfish, self-centered, and in some ways brutish. It seems like the four walls of the class only teach men to raise themselves by stomping on others; make themselves wise by making others seem foolish.

The four walls of the classroom and the system employed by the school have taught a lot of us the paradigms that keep men poor. The worst case is; that we rank our whole lives by the ranking the school stats have given us.

Those who are called 'smart' will keep doing what made them smart in school; even when they realize it doesn't work, they just stick to it – what a detrimental loyalty! Those who are termed 'dull' (I feel we should pity them, but I won't be different from the system I am trying to correct if I do) will continue to look down on themselves; running around with low self-esteem, feeling short at all times and seeming dejected. These unlike their 'smart' colleagues jump at any available job just to put food on their tables. The system that makes winners and losers automatically made losers of everyone.

If we can change it all, why don't we? Why should we stick to the system that makes a

lot of people fall below the poverty line?
Even those we call rich are lacking wealth –
just as Mo Salah cannot defend or
goal-keep. If we want this world to change
from a place of prevailing poverty to a place
where wealth is popular, even among
minority people; then we need to change
ourselves. We need to change the system
that teaches us about life, we need to change
the system employed by the agent of
socialization called 'SCHOOL' – it seems
like it is the biggest of poverty propagation.

*"Any fool can make money.  A wealthy
person knows how to spend it"*
                     - Robert Kiyosaki

"I will instruct you and teach you the way
you should go"
                     - Proverbs 32:8

NOTE: The school system seems to groom us all to become fools, but most of us find it very difficult to create wealth; some others find it impossible, and only a few truly make wealth. The school taught us to keep up with the Joneses, to be 'smart' — sorry, 'to look smart'. We don't want people who look wealthy, not anymore; we want a truly wealthy society, where assets in all ways outnumber liabilities.

**Chapter 9**

*SAPA*
*Nice One!*

*"SAPA"* - /sa:pa:/
Origin: Nigeria; the Yoruba tribe, the streets
of the country (early 21st Century)

Meaning: A condition of lack of financial
capacity to get one's other needs met.

Noun – a state in one's life where there is a
total lack of money; and due to this, there is
a negative emotional implication.

Noun – a lack of power or personae that
represents a lack.

Synonyms: Poverty, Impoverish, Lack,
Beggary, Destituteness, Penury

It was in 2020, right after the CoronaVirus pandemic which caused a lockdown across the nation. The lockdown lasted for about 12 weeks and a lot of people who had businesses were forced to either shut down their businesses or run the business at a loss. This condition caused a lot of people to be impoverished, poor, or in lack. The slang, whose source no one can tell, became a trend. Everyone began to use the *SAPA* slang and the condition itself became a thing in vogue.

To bring the whole book home, I'll tell you a story.

When I was nine, I lived with my dad and my stepmom – socially, that is what she was. My dad was always traveling from state to state. On this particular occasion, he traveled to Zamfara State; he was working on a building project, and he thought the trip would take him only 21 days to return. We expected the worst-case scenario, that he would be back in four weeks. As usual, he dropped our money to cater for feeding expenses and other things that pertain to our upkeep.

After three weeks, all the money we were spending seem to be gone, we were only living on extra with the hope that dad's return was imminent; yet, at four weeks, dad hadn't returned. It was a stringent, tough, and hunger-filled season, but we tried to manage. Eventually, my stepmom resumed her hair dressing business; and she returns home later than 8 pm on most days. I didn't know her shop, so I didn't have a way to access her when she was not around.

On a fateful day, I was really hungry and nothing was available. I looked around; since begging was the last thing I wanted to do, I summoned a little courage, and found a relaxation center around us, it was a beer parlor. I went there to do a few songs I previously scored, knowing fully well that if they are impressed by my performance, I would get a good financial reward. My plan worked; I got a few naira, maybe a little above a hundred naira. I was so pleased with my achievement that I began to strategize when to visit the beer parlor again, do my singing and earn some more money. I hid it from my stepmom, but I was sure I couldn't do that for long. My dad had not returned after about eight weeks; this meant all I could depend on was a late dinner from my stepmom and a very light breakfast. I could as well depend on my singing skill, do my music at beer parlors, and earn some money (at least that will cover lunch and snacks).

This went on until my stepmom found out about my 'beer parlor' mission; she was offended, she thought I was trying to give her a bad face in the locality, so, my 'business' was stopped. I became dependent on her again, the truth was; that my feeding term improved, but it still wasn't like it was when I was earning my cash. Dad returned and everything reverted to normal.

Many societies kick against child labor, but it isn't child labor if the child loves the job he is doing. It isn't child labor, if the child has adults who cater to his wellbeing, give him the right education, and do it in a good condition. Many a child, have we stopped from fulfilling our purpose because we thought going to school is all that matters. We allow our archaic paradigm to affect the unexplored future of the coming generations. We allow ourselves to earn a 'good face' to the detriment of teaching our future leaders how wealth can be gotten. No wonder *SAPA* has a huge grip on many today.

The most important inspiration for this book is not prosperity, it is the hatred for lack. We convince ourselves that the 'love of money is the root of all evil' and we quickly forget that "money answereth all things".

We do not remember that 'money is a defense' and that the "rich rule over the poor".

It seems 'education' – since that is what we call what we do, has failed us. But we stick to that failure because we don't want to be socially wrong. A man, Isaac, was said to have sowed in a land of famine when others were running to other lands, looking around for greener pastures, seeking who to help them earn plants for food. Many even blamed their lack on the drought, and by so doing, they shut down their creativity, they left their opportunities behind.

Issac, on the other hand, reaped in folds of hundreds; he became a wealthy man. He was termed alongside nations; he became an inventor – yes, an inventor in irrigation farming. He became truly great. The school didn't teach him that, he was initially socially wrong, but in the very end, his methods paid off.

If we stick to this 'memorize the answers', 'know these methods', 'follow this pattern'; we would be in for a shock, and poverty will be the name that rules both those who have money and those who don't.

I, therefore, call us to action; I say we stop the wrong/right methods of the school curriculum. I say we stop terming those who don't know what we teach them as 'dull'. I say we give our kids the opportunity to explore fields they never knew or no one has ever tried. I say we encourage personalized learning so everyone can learn what he wants when he wants and how he wants. I say we encourage mistakes because that is how success is born. I say we quit the 'blame game' and take responsibility. Remember, those who are wealthy now were once in one mess or the other. If the mind can change, the state of the pocket can too. If the logic can change, liabilities can diminish too.

Check the stats on poverty, and you will see that not less than 33% of citizens of this country live far below the poverty line; not more than 10% of this country's population live in wealth that could last 100+ years; not less than 50% of this same population are dependent – on a boss, on a paid job, on family members, on government, on spouses and many others. This must stop! We need to look at our future with hope from hence; and not despair. Do not forget, you could say *SAPA, NICE ONE!* And mean it from a wealth perspective.

### *SCHOOL NO BE SCAM, Na the method dey SCAM us!*

www.ingramcontent.com/pod-product-compliance
Lightning Source LLC
Chambersburg PA
CBHW050035260726
48658CB00005B/1617